THE KITCHEN LIBRARY
COOKING FOR TWO

THE KITCHEN LIBRARY

COOKING FOR TWO

Rhona Newman

HAMLYN

CONTENTS

This edition published 1991 by
The Hamlyn Publishing Group Limited
part of Reed International Books
Michelin House
81 Fulham Road
London SW3 6RB

© Copyright Reed International Books Limited 1980
ISBN 0 600 57262 5

Produced by Mandarin Offset
Printed in Hong Kong

INTRODUCTION

Whether you are cooking for one, two or a large family, it is equally important to serve appetizing meals. Often there is less incentive to cook proper meals for small numbers and a tendency to reach for cans and packets or rush for a 'take away'.

The exciting new cookbook is especially designed to provide nutritious, attractive dishes for two, with quantities carefully chosen to avoid wastage. There are recipes suitable for all occasions, from quick snack lunches to intimate dinner parties for two.

Certain dishes, including Turkey fricassée, Crispy sage lamb and Orange pasta salad, are based on cooked ingredients, making excellent use of leftovers.

Most of the recipes are quick and easy to make, others may require a little forward planning. Whatever the occasion this practical cookbook will provide a source of inspiration when cooking for two.

NOTES

Standard spoon measurements are used in all recipes
1 tablespoon = one 15 ml spoon
1 teaspoon = one 5 ml spoon
All spoon measures are level.

Fresh herbs are used unless otherwise stated. If unobtainable substitute a bouquet garni of the equivalent dried herbs, or use dried herbs instead but halve the quantities stated.

Use freshly ground black pepper where pepper is specified.

Ovens should be preheated to the specified temperature.

For all recipes, quantities are given in both metric and imperial measures. Follow either set but not a mixture of both, because they are not interchangeable.

All recipes serve 2 unless otherwise stated.

Tangy Grapefruit

1 grapefruit, halved
2-3 tablespoons
   raisins
4 tablespoons natural
   low-fat yogurt
1-2 tablespoons
   brown sugar
   (optional)

Cut the segments from each grapefruit half, discarding the pith and reserving the shells. Place the segments in a bowl and stir in the raisins and yogurt.

Pile the mixture into the grapefruit shells and sprinkle with sugar, if preferred. Chill in the refrigerator overnight.

Bran Yogurt

1 banana, sliced
150 g (5 oz)
   mandarin yogurt
1-2 tablespoons
   chopped hazelnuts
2 tablespoons bran

Divide the banana between two bowls. Top with the yogurt and sprinkle with the hazelnuts and bran.

Muesli

4 tablespoons
   porridge oats
2 tablespoons
   grapenuts
2 tablespoons
   sultanas
1 tablespoon brown
   sugar
1 tablespoon mixed
   nuts, toasted
150-300 ml
   (¼-½ pint) milk
   to serve

Place the porridge oats, grapenuts, sultanas, sugar and nuts in a bowl. Mix well and divide between 2 serving dishes. Add the milk just before serving.

Cereal Medley

2 wholewheat bisks,
   crushed
25 g (1 oz)
   cornflakes
3 tablespoons
   All-Bran
½ dessert apple,
   peeled, cored and
   grated
2 teaspoons brown
   sugar
2 tablespoons fruit
   yogurt
milk to serve

Place all the ingredients except the
yogurt and milk in a bowl. Mix well
and divide between 2 serving dishes.
Spoon the yogurt over and serve
with milk.

9

Milk and Orange Nog

300 ml (½ pint)
  chilled milk
1 egg
2 tablespoons
  mandarin yogurt
grated rind and juice
  of 1 orange
1 teaspoon honey
grated nutmeg

Whisk together the milk and egg, then add the yogurt, orange rind, juice and honey. Continue whisking until well blended.

Pour into tumblers and sprinkle with nutmeg to taste.

Kipper Toast

1 x 175 g (6 oz)
  packet kipper
  fillets with butter
grated rind and juice
  of 1 lemon
1 tablespoon chopped
  parsley
pepper
2 slices wholemeal
  bread, toasted
parsley sprigs to
  garnish

Cook the kipper fillets according to the packet instructions.

Place the fish in a bowl and mash with a fork. Add the lemon rind, juice, parsley and pepper to taste. Mix well, then divide the mixture between the toast slices.

Place under a preheated medium grill for 4 to 5 minutes. Garnish with parsley sprigs and serve immediately.

Beany Breakfast

1 x 219 g (7¾ oz)
  can baked beans
1 hard-boiled egg,
  chopped
50 g (2 oz) cooked
  ham, chopped
1 teaspoon
  Worcestershire
  sauce
½ teaspoon made
  mustard
2 teaspoons tomato
  ketchup
salt and pepper
2 slices bread, toasted
15 g (½ oz) butter

Place the beans in a saucepan with the egg, ham, Worcestershire sauce, mustard and tomato ketchup. Heat gently and add salt and pepper to taste.

Spread the toast with the butter and pile the bean mixture on top. Serve immediately.

Onion and Tomato Scramble

3 eggs
2 tablespoons single
  cream
salt and pepper
25 g (1 oz) butter
½ small onion,
  finely chopped
1 tomato, skinned
  and chopped
2 slices bread, toasted

Beat the eggs with the cream and salt and pepper to taste.

Melt half the butter in a small saucepan, add the onion and fry until soft. Pour in the egg mixture and stir slowly over a gentle heat until scrambled. Stir in the tomato and remove from the heat.

Spread the toast with the remaining butter and pile the scrambled egg mixture on top. Serve immediately.

Lancashire Baps

15 g (½ oz) butter
125 g (4 oz)
    Lancashire cheese,
    grated
½ teaspoon French
    mustard
1 teaspoon milk
salt and pepper
2 baps
1 tomato, skinned
    and sliced
parsley sprigs to
    garnish

Melt the butter in a saucepan and add the cheese. Cook over a low heat, stirring, until the cheese has melted. Stir in the mustard, milk and salt and pepper to taste.

Slice the baps in half and toast the cut side. Spread with the cheese mixture and top with the tomato slices. Place under a preheated medium grill for 2 to 3 minutes. Garnish with parsley. Serve immediately.

Sausage Parcels

4 pork sausages
English mustard
50 g (2 oz) Cheddar
    cheese
2 streaky bacon
    rashers, derinded
    and halved

Cook the sausages under a preheated medium grill for 10 to 15 minutes, turning to brown evenly. Spread with mustard to taste.

Cut the cheese into 4 strips and press onto the sausages. Wrap a piece of bacon around each sausage.

Return to the grill and cook for a further 10 minutes, turning once.

Serve with grilled tomatoes or baked beans.

FISH

Mackerel with Gooseberries

2 mackerel, filleted
1 tablespoon fine
    oatmeal
salt and pepper
knob of butter
SAUCE:
125 g (4 oz)
    gooseberries
1 tablespoon water
1 teaspoon sugar
pinch of grated
    nutmeg

Rinse and dry the mackerel fillets. Season the oatmeal with salt and pepper to taste and sprinkle over the mackerel. Dot with butter and cook under a preheated medium grill for 15 to 20 minutes.

To make the sauce: Put all the ingredients in a saucepan. Cover and simmer for 10 to 15 minutes until the fruit is soft.

Cool slightly, then rub through a sieve or work in an electric blender until smooth and strain to remove pips.

Place the mackerel on a warmed serving dish. Pour over the sauce. Serve immediately.

Haddock with Sour Cream and Mushrooms

300 g (10 oz)
   haddock fillet
salt and pepper
knob of butter
4 tablespoons water
SAUCE:
15 g (½ oz) butter
50 g (2 oz) button
   mushrooms, sliced
120 ml (4 fl oz)
   fresh sour cream
¼ teaspoon paprika
TO GARNISH:
chopped parsley

Place the haddock in a shallow 600 ml (1 pint) ovenproof dish. Sprinkle with salt and pepper, dot with the butter and add the water. Cover with foil and cook in a preheated moderate oven, 160°C (325°F), Gas Mark 3, for 20 minutes.

Meanwhile, make the sauce: Melt the butter in a saucepan, add the mushrooms and fry for 1 minute. Stir in the sour cream, paprika and salt and pepper to taste. Heat through gently.

Drain the fish and transfer to a warmed serving dish. Pour over the sauce and garnish with chopped parsley. Serve immediately.

Cod with Lemon and Watercress Sauce

2 cod steaks
1 small onion, sliced
1 bay leaf
4 black peppercorns
grated rind of
  ½ lemon
3 tablespoons dry
  cider
salt and pepper
SAUCE:
2 teaspoons cornflour
1 teaspoon lemon
  juice
1 egg yolk
4 tablespoons milk
½ bunch watercress,
  stalks removed
TO GARNISH:
watercress sprigs

Place the cod in a shallow 600 ml (1 pint) ovenproof dish. Add the onion, bay leaf, peppercorns, lemon rind, cider and salt to taste. Cover with foil and cook in a preheated moderate oven, 160°C (325°F), Gas Mark 3, for 20 minutes.

Transfer the fish to a warmed serving dish, discarding any skin and bones; keep hot. Strain the fish liquor and add water if necessary to make up to 5 tablespoons; cool. Blend the cornflour with the fish liquor and lemon juice. Heat, stirring, until thickened. Beat the egg yolk and milk together, then add to the sauce.

Finely chop the watercress leaves. Add to the sauce with salt and pepper to taste. Heat gently but do not boil.

Pour the sauce over the fish. Serve immediately, garnished with watercress.

Plaice with Banana and Nuts

300 g (10 oz) plaice
  fillet
15 g (½ oz) butter
1 banana, sliced
25 g (1 oz) peanuts
25 g (1 oz) Cheddar
  cheese, grated
SAUCE:
15 g (½ oz) butter
2 tablespoons plain
  flour
150 ml (¼ pint)
  milk
2 tablespoons natural
  low-fat yogurt
salt and pepper
TO GARNISH:
parsley sprigs

Place the fish in a greased shallow ovenproof dish. Dot with the butter and cook in a preheated moderate oven, 180°C (350°F), Gas Mark 4, for 10 minutes. Remove from the oven and arrange the banana and nuts over the fish.

To make the sauce: Melt the butter in a saucepan and stir in the flour. Cook for 1 minute, then gradually blend in the milk. Heat, stirring until the sauce thickens. Stir in the yogurt, with salt and pepper to taste.

Pour the sauce over the fish, sprinkle with the cheese and return to the oven for 15 minutes.

Garnish with parsley. Serve immediately.

Herb Fish Cakes

*300 g (10 oz)
   potatoes, chopped
1 small onion, sliced
salt and pepper
1 tablespoon milk
15 g (½ oz) butter
250 g (8 oz) white
   fish fillet, skinned
   and chopped
2 teaspoons chopped
   parsley
½ teaspoon dried
   mixed herbs
1 egg, separated
dry breadcrumbs for
   coating
oil for shallow frying
parsley sprigs to
   garnish*

Cook the potatoes and onion in boiling salted water until soft. Drain and mash, then beat in the milk.

Melt the butter in a saucepan, add the fish and fry for 10 to 15 minutes or until tender. Flake the fish and add to the potato. Stir in the herbs, egg yolk and salt and pepper to taste. Mix well, then leave to cool.

On a floured surface, divide the mixture into 4 and shape each piece into a flat cake. Lightly beat the egg white. Dip the fish cakes into the egg white, then coat with breadcrumbs.

Heat the oil in a frying pan and fry the fish cakes until crisp and golden. Transfer to a warmed serving dish and garnish with parsley. Serve immediately.

17

Kipper Vol-au-Vent

½ x 212 g (7½ oz)
  packet frozen puff
  pastry, thawed
75 g (3 oz) kipper
  fillets
15 g (½ oz) butter
2 tablespoons plain
  flour
150 ml (¼ pint)
  milk
40 g (1½ oz)
  Cheddar cheese,
  grated
2 teaspoons chopped
  parsley
salt and pepper

Roll out the pastry to a 15 cm
(6 inch) circle. Using an 8.5 cm
(3½ inch) cutter, mark a circle in the
centre, cutting halfway through the
pastry.

Place on a baking sheet and cook
in a preheated hot oven, 220°C
(425°F), Gas Mark 7, for 20 minutes.

Cook the kipper fillets under a
preheated medium grill for 2 to 3
minutes on each side, then flake.

Melt the butter in a saucepan and
stir in the flour. Cook for 1 minute,
then gradually blend in the milk.
Heat, stirring, until the sauce
thickens. Stir in the fish, cheese,
parsley and salt and pepper to taste.
Heat gently, stirring, until the cheese
has melted.

When cooked, ease out the
vol-au-vent lid and discard any soft
pastry in the centre. Fill the case with
the kipper mixture and replace the
lid. Serve hot.

Crispy Tangy Fish

15 g (¹/2 oz) butter
2 tablespoons plain
  flour
150 ml (¹/4 pint)
  milk
1 tablespoon salad
  cream
¹/2 teaspoon lemon
  juice
salt and pepper
250 g (8 oz) white
  fish fillet
25 g (1 oz) dry
  breadcrumbs
25 g (1 oz) streaky
  bacon, derinded
  and chopped
25 g (1 oz) Cheddar
  cheese, grated
TO GARNISH:
tomato slices

Melt the butter in a saucepan, stir in the flour and cook for 1 minute. Gradually blend in the milk and heat, stirring, until the sauce thickens. Stir in the salad cream, lemon juice and salt and pepper to taste.

Divide the fish into 2 pieces, place in a shallow ovenproof dish and pour over the sauce. Combine the breadcrumbs, bacon and cheese and sprinkle over the sauce.

Cook in a preheated moderately hot oven, 190°C (375°F), Gas Mark 5, for 20 minutes, then place under a preheated medium grill for 2 to 3 minutes to brown the topping.

Garnish with tomato slices. Serve immediately.

Pilchard and Egg Supper

1 x 227 g (8 oz) can
  pilchards in
  tomatoes
1 hard-boiled egg
1 celery stick,
  chopped
50 g (2 oz) frozen
  peas
4 tablespoons milk
  (approximately)
15 g (½ oz) butter
2 tablespoons plain
  flour
pinch of sugar
salt and pepper
½ x 25 g (1 oz)
  packet potato
  crisps, crushed
chopped parsley to
  garnish

Drain the pilchards, reserving the
juice. Arrange the pilchards in a
shallow ovenproof dish. Cut the egg
into quarters and place in the dish.
Scatter the celery and peas over the
top.

Make the pilchard juice up to
150 ml (¼ pint) with the milk.

Melt the butter in a saucepan and
stir in the flour. Cook for 1 minute,
then gradually blend in the liquid.
Heat, stirring, until the sauce
thickens. Add the sugar and salt and
pepper to taste.

Pour the sauce over the fish,
sprinkle with the crisps and cook in a
preheated moderate oven, 180°C
(350°F), Gas Mark 4, for 30 minutes.

Garnish with parsley. Serve
immediately.

Stuffed Haddock Parcels

2 tablespoons parsley
  and thyme stuffing
  mix
4 tablespoons boiling
  water
25 g (1 oz) Cheddar
  cheese, grated
salt and pepper
2 haddock steaks
knob of butter
SAUCE:
1 tablespoon
  mayonnaise (see
  page 73)
1 tablespoon natural
  low-fat yogurt
1 teaspoon finely
  chopped parsley
¼ teaspoon dried
  thyme
TO GARNISH:
watercress sprigs

Place the stuffing mix in a bowl and
add the boiling water. Stir in the
cheese and salt and pepper to taste.

Place each haddock steak on a
piece of foil and top with the
stuffing. Dot with the butter and
fold the foil, enclosing the filling, to
make parcels.

Place the parcels on a baking sheet
and cook in a preheated moderately
hot oven, 190°C (375°F), Gas Mark
5, for 20 to 25 minutes. Fold back the
foil and continue to cook for 5 to 10
minutes until the topping is golden.

Blend all the sauce ingredients
together, with salt and pepper to
taste. Transfer the fish to a warmed
serving dish. Garnish with
watercress and serve the sauce
separately.

Potato Cod Bake

300 g (10 oz) cod
    fillet
½ small onion,
    finely chopped
3 black peppercorns
1 small dessert apple,
    peeled, cored and
    sliced
salt and pepper
¼ teaspoon dried
    thyme
4 tablespoons dry
    cider
4-5 tablespoons milk
15 g (½ oz) butter
2 tablespoons plain
    flour
TOPPING:
1 x 85 g (3 oz)
    packet instant
    potato
300 ml (½ pint)
    boiling water
1 tablespoon milk
knob of butter
grated nutmeg

Place the cod, onion, peppercorns, apple, salt, thyme and cider in a buttered 900 ml (1½ pint) ovenproof dish. Cover and cook in a preheated moderate oven, 160°C (325°F), Gas Mark 3, for 20 minutes.

Strain the fish liquor and make up to 150 ml (¼ pint) with the milk. Melt the butter in a saucepan and stir in the flour. Cook for 1 minute, then gradually blend in the fish liquor. Heat, stirring until the sauce thickens. Add salt and pepper to taste.

Flake the fish and add to the sauce with the onion and apple. Heat through gently and transfer to the buttered ovenproof dish.

Make up the potato with the boiling water as directed on the packet. Beat in the milk and butter. Add nutmeg, salt and pepper to taste.

Spread the potato over the fish and mark a pattern on top with a fork. Place under a preheated medium grill for 2 to 3 minutes. Serve immediately.

Salmon Mousse

2 teaspoons gelatine
150 ml (¼ pint)
　water
150 ml (¼ pint)
　single cream
2 eggs, separated
1 teaspoon lemon
　juice
½ teaspoon anchovy
　essence
salt and pepper
1 x 212 g (7½ oz)
　can salmon,
　drained
TO GARNISH:
cucumber slices
parsley sprigs

Sprinkle the gelatine over the water in a bowl. Place over a saucepan of gently simmering water and stir until dissolved. Cool slightly.

Warm the cream, then beat in the egg yolks. Mix in the dissolved gelatine with the lemon juice, anchovy essence and salt and pepper to taste.

Remove any skin and bones, then mash the salmon until smooth. Add to the egg and cream mixture and mix until thoroughly blended.

Whisk the egg whites until they form soft peaks. Fold into the salmon mixture. Transfer to a 600 ml (1 pint) soufflé dish and chill until set.

Serve garnished with cucumber and parsley.

Tuna Pasta Salad

125 g (4 oz) pasta
　shells
salt and pepper
50 g (2 oz) button
　mushrooms, sliced
½ green pepper,
　cored, seeded and
　chopped
1 x 227 g (8 oz) can
　tomatoes, drained
　and chopped
1 x 99 g (3½ oz)
　can tuna, drained
　and flaked
2 teaspoons oil
1 teaspoon lemon
　juice
garlic salt
chopped parsley to
　garnish

Cook the pasta in plenty of boiling salted water until al dente (tender but still firm to the bite). Drain and rinse thoroughly under cold running water.

Place the pasta in a serving bowl and add the mushrooms, green pepper, tomatoes and tuna.

Blend the oil with the lemon juice, then add garlic salt and pepper to taste. Pour the dressing over the pasta and toss well.

Garnish with parsley before serving.

NOTE: The flavour improves if this dish is prepared the day before required and left in the refrigerator overnight.

Lamb in Redcurrant and Mint Sauce

2 lamb chops
salt and pepper
15 g (½ oz) butter
1 small onion, sliced
1 tablespoon plain
  flour
150 ml (¼ pint)
  stock
2 teaspoons
  redcurrant jelly
1 teaspoon mint
  sauce
pinch of sugar
1 tablespoon single
  cream (optional)
mint sprigs to garnish

Trim the chops and sprinkle with salt and pepper. Melt half the butter in a frying pan, add the chops and cook for 10 to 15 minutes on each side. Drain and transfer to a warmed serving dish. Keep hot.

Melt the remaining butter in the pan, add the onion and fry until soft. Stir in the flour and cook for 1 minute. Gradually blend in the stock and heat, stirring, until the sauce thickens.

Add the redcurrant jelly, mint sauce, sugar and salt and pepper to taste. Stir in the cream, if used. Pour the sauce over the chops and garnish with mint.

Serve with new potatoes and peas.

Lamb Hotpot

500 g (1 lb) middle
  neck of lamb
250 g (8 oz)
  potatoes, sliced
salt and pepper
1 onion, sliced
2 carrots, sliced
1 celery stick,
  chopped
½ teaspoon dried
  mixed herbs
200 ml (⅓ pint)
  stock
15 g (½ oz) butter,
  melted

Divide the lamb into cutlets.

Cover the base of a 1.2 litre (2 pint) casserole dish with half the potatoes. Arrange the lamb on top and sprinkle liberally with salt and pepper.

Mix together the onion, carrots, celery and herbs, with salt and pepper to taste. Spread over the lamb. Pour over the stock. Arrange the remaining potatoes in overlapping circles on top and brush with the butter.

Cover and cook in a preheated moderate oven, 180°C (350°F), Gas Mark 4, for 1½ hours. Remove the lid and continue to cook for 20 to 30 minutes until the potatoes are browned.

Lamb Parcels

2 lamb chops
salt and pepper
15 g (½ oz) butter
½ x 212 g (7½ oz)
   packet frozen puff
   pastry, thawed
50 g (2 oz) liver
   pâté
beaten egg to glaze
watercress sprigs to
   garnish

Sprinkle the chops with salt and pepper. Melt the butter in a frying pan, add the chops and brown on both sides. Lower the heat and cook for 10 to 15 minutes. Drain on kitchen paper. Cool slightly.

Roll out the pastry to a rectangle about 30 x 15 cm (12 x 6 inches), then cut in half to make two squares.

Spread the chops with the pâté, and place, pâté side down, on the pastry squares. Brush the pastry edges with water. Fold the pastry over the chops and press the edges together to seal. Place on a baking sheet, with the seams underneath. Decorate with pastry leaves cut from the trimmings. Brush with egg.

Cook in a preheated hot oven, 220°C (425°F), Gas Mark 7, for 15 minutes. Lower the temperature to moderate, 180°C (350°F), Gas Mark 4, and cook for 15 to 20 minutes.

Transfer to a warmed serving dish and garnish with watercress.

Crispy Sage Lamb

15 g (¹/2 oz) butter
¹/2 onion, chopped
1 tablespoon onion
    soup powder
150 ml (¹/4 pint)
    milk
300 g (10 oz) cold
    cooked lamb,
    chopped
¹/2 x 95 g (3¹/2 oz)
    packet sage and
    onion stuffing mix
150 ml (¹/4 pint)
    boiling water
¹/2 teaspoon dried
    sage
25 g (1 oz)
    Lancashire cheese,
    grated
salt and pepper
1 tomato, sliced, to
    garnish

Melt the butter in a saucepan, add the onion and fry until soft. Stir in the soup powder, then gradually blend in the milk. Heat, stirring, until the sauce thickens. Add the lamb and cook until heated through.

Make up the stuffing with the boiling water as directed on the packet. Stir in the sage, cheese and salt and pepper to taste.

Place the lamb in a warmed, greased 600 ml (1 pint) ovenproof dish. Spoon the stuffing over the top and place under a preheated hot grill until the topping is crisp and brown.

Garnish with tomato slices. Serve immediately.

Beef with Orange

1 ½ tablespoons plain
    flour
salt and pepper
350 g (12 oz) chuck
    steak, cubed
15 g (½ oz) butter
1 small onion,
    chopped
½ green pepper,
    cored, seeded and
    chopped
grated rind and juice
    of 1 small orange
200 ml (⅓ pint) beef
    stock
2 tablespoons orange
    squash
chopped parsley to
    garnish

Season the flour with salt and pepper
and use to coat the meat. Melt the
butter in a pan, add the onion and
pepper and fry until soft. Add the
meat and fry, turning, until evenly
browned. Transfer to a 900 ml
(1½ pint) casserole dish.

Stir in the orange rind and juice,
stock and orange squash, with salt
and pepper to taste. Cover and cook
in a preheated moderate oven, 160°C
(325°F), Gas Mark 3, for 1 to 1¼
hours.

Serve hot, garnished with parsley.

Beef Crumble

250 g (8 oz) minced
  beef
1 small onion, finely
  chopped
1 celery stick, chopped
25 g (1 oz) mush-
  rooms, chopped
1 small carrot, grated
1 teaspoon plain flour
150 ml (¼ pint) beef
  stock
½ teaspoon Worcester-
  shire sauce
salt and pepper
TOPPING:
75 g (3 oz)
  wholewheat flour
25 g (1 oz) porridge
  oats
25 g (1 oz) butter
40 g (1½ oz)
  Cheddar cheese,
  grated
½ teaspoon dried
  mixed herbs
TO GARNISH:
parsley sprigs

Place a frying pan over moderate heat. Add the minced beef and fry in its own fat, turning, until evenly browned. Add the onion, celery, mushrooms and carrot and fry for 5 minutes. Stir in the flour and cook for 1 minute. Add the stock, Worcestershire sauce and salt and pepper to taste. Bring to the boil, stirring. Cover and simmer for 30 to 40 minutes.

To make the topping: Place the flour and oats in a bowl. Rub in the butter until the mixture resembles coarse breadcrumbs. Stir in the cheese, herbs and salt and pepper to taste.

Transfer the meat to a greased 600 ml (1 pint) ovenproof dish and spoon the topping over. Cook in a preheated moderately hot oven, 190°C (375°F), Gas Mark 5, for 20 to 30 minutes.

Serve hot, garnished with parsley.

Chilli Beef

50 g (2 oz) dried red
  kidney beans
350 g (12 oz)
  minced beef
1 onion, finely
  chopped
½ small green
  pepper, cored,
  seeded and
  chopped
1 x 227 g (8 oz) can
  tomatoes
2 tablespoons water
½-1 teaspoon chilli
  powder
½ teaspoon cumin
  seeds
salt and pepper

Place the beans in a bowl and cover with cold water. Leave to soak overnight then drain, rinse and place in a saucepan. Cover with fresh cold water. Bring to the boil and boil steadily for 10 minutes. Lower the heat, cover and simmer for 25 minutes, then drain.

Place a frying pan over moderate heat. Add the minced beef and fry in its own fat, turning, until evenly browned. Add the onion and pepper and fry for 5 minutes. Stir in the tomatoes with their juice, water, chilli powder, cumin and salt and pepper to taste.

Bring to the boil, stirring, then add the beans. Cover and simmer for 1 hour. Spoon into 2 hot serving bowls. Serve hot, with a green salad and pitta bread, if liked.

Hamburgers with Barbecue Sauce

250 g (8 oz) lean
  minced beef
2 teaspoons finely
  chopped onion
1/2 teaspoon made
  mustard
2 teaspoons chopped
  parsley
salt and pepper
15 g (1/2 oz) butter,
  melted
SAUCE:
15 g (1/2 oz) butter
1 onion, finely
  chopped
1 tablespoon tomato
  ketchup
1 tablespoon vinegar
3 teaspoons brown
  sugar
pinch of chilli
  powder
1/2 teaspoon dry
  mustard
1/2 teaspoon dried
  mixed herbs
6 tablespoons water

Place the minced beef, onion, mustard and parsley in a bowl. Add salt and pepper to taste and mix well. Divide the mixture into 4 and shape each piece into a flat cake.

To make the sauce: Melt the butter in a small saucepan, add the onion and fry until soft. Combine the remaining ingredients, mix thoroughly, then add to the pan. Bring to the boil, cover and simmer for 20 minutes.

Brush the hamburgers with the melted butter and cook under a preheated hot grill for 8 to 10 minutes, turning once.

Transfer to a warmed serving dish. Serve hot, with French fried potatoes and French beans or peas. Hand the sauce separately.

Devonshire Pork Casserole

15 g (½ oz) lard
1 small onion, sliced
1 clove garlic,
    crushed
350 g (12 oz) pork
    fillet, cubed
2 teaspoons plain
    flour
150 ml (¼ pint)
    cider
3 tablespoons stock
½ teaspoon dried
    sage
salt and pepper
1 small cooking
    apple, peeled,
    cored and sliced
    into rings
2 tablespoons single
    cream

Melt the lard in a pan, add the onion and garlic and fry until soft. Add the pork and fry, turning, until evenly browned. Transfer the pork and onion to a 1.2 litre (2 pint) casserole dish, using a slotted spoon.

Add the flour to the fat remaining in the pan and cook for 1 minute. Gradually blend in the cider and stock and heat, stirring, until the sauce thickens.

Stir in the sage and salt and pepper to taste. Arrange the apple slices in the casserole dish and pour over the sauce. Cover and cook in a preheated moderate oven, 180°C (350°F), Gas Mark 4, for 1½ hours.

Add the cream and serve immediately.

Pork with Prunes

6 prunes
1 teaspoon lemon
    juice
1 tablespoon plain
    flour
salt and pepper
2 pork chops, boned
15 g (½ oz) butter
1 teaspoon oil
150 ml (¼ pint) dry
    cider
2 teaspoons
    redcurrant jelly
4 tablespoons double
    cream
chopped parsley to
    garnish

Place the prunes in a bowl and cover with cold water. Add the lemon juice and leave to soak overnight.

Season the flour with salt and pepper and use to coat the meat. Heat the butter and oil in a flameproof casserole. Add the chops and fry for 5 minutes on each side. Add the cider, cover and simmer for 30 minutes or until the pork is tender.

Cook the prunes in the soaking liquid for 20 minutes or until tender.

Transfer the meat and prunes to a warmed serving dish, using a slotted spoon; keep hot. Add 3 tablespoons of the prune liquid to the casserole. Stir well and simmer until the sauce is reduced and thickened.

Stir in the redcurrant jelly and cream. Heat gently, then pour over the pork. Garnish with parsley and serve immediately.

Pork with Orange and Apricots

15 g (½ oz) butter
2 pork chops
grated rind and juice
  of ½ orange
salt and pepper
1 small onion, finely
  chopped
½ green pepper,
  cored, seeded and
  chopped
200 ml (⅓ pint)
  stock
1 teaspoon cornflour
pinch of sugar
50 g (2 oz) dried
  apricots
watercress sprigs to
  garnish

Melt the butter in a frying pan. Add the chops and fry on both sides until evenly browned.

Transfer to a shallow ovenproof dish, using a slotted spoon. Sprinkle with the orange rind and salt and pepper to taste.

Add the onion and pepper to the fat remaining in the pan and fry until soft. Stir in the stock. Blend the cornflour with the orange juice and add to the pan. Heat, stirring, until the sauce thickens. Add the sugar and salt and pepper to taste.

Arrange the apricots on top of the pork and pour over the sauce. Cover with foil and cook in a preheated moderate oven, 180°C (350°F), Gas Mark 4, for 1 to 1¼ hours.

Serve hot, garnished with watercress.

Honey and Apricot Ham

40 g (1 ½ oz) dried
  apricots
½ teaspoon made
  mustard
1 teaspoon honey
salt and pepper
2 ham steaks
2 teaspoons cornflour
½ chicken stock
  cube, crumbled
parsley sprigs to
  garnish

Place the apricots in a bowl and cover with cold water. Leave to soak for 2 to 3 hours.

Mix together the mustard, honey and pepper to taste. Spread this mixture over both sides of the ham steaks. Cook under a preheated medium grill for 6 to 8 minutes on each side.

Drain the apricots, reserving the liquid; make this up to 150 ml (¼ pint) with water if necessary. Blend the cornflour with a little of the liquid, then stir in the remainder.

Pour into a saucepan and heat, stirring, until the sauce thickens. Add the stock cube and apricots and simmer for 1 minute. Check the seasoning.

Place the ham steaks on a warmed serving dish and pour over the sauce. Garnish with parsley. Serve immediately.

Sausage and Black-Eyed Bean Casserole

*50 g (2 oz)
    black-eyed beans
6 large pork sausages
1 small onion, finely
    chopped
1 x 227 g (8 oz) can
    tomatoes
4 tablespoons water
½ beef stock cube,
    crumbled
½ teaspoon dried
    mixed herbs
salt and pepper*

Place the beans in a bowl, cover with cold water and leave to soak overnight. Drain, rinse and place the beans in a saucepan. Cover with fresh cold water, bring to the boil and simmer for 45 minutes or until tender. Drain.

Cook the sausages under a preheated medium grill, turning frequently, until evenly browned. Cool slightly, then cut into 1 cm (½ inch) pieces. Place in a 1.2 litre (2 pint) casserole dish.

Add the beans, onion, tomatoes with their juice, water, stock cube, herbs and salt and pepper to taste. Mix well. Cover and cook in a preheated moderate oven, 180°C (350°F), Gas Mark 4, for 45 minutes.

Serve hot, with jacket potatoes.

Italian Veal Casserole

1 tablespoon oil
350 g (12 oz) lean
  veal, cubed
1 clove garlic,
  crushed
1 small onion, sliced
1/2 green pepper,
  cored, seeded and
  chopped
125 g (4 oz)
  tomatoes, skinned
  and chopped
200 ml (1/3 pint)
  light stock
salt and pepper
1 bouquet garni
chopped parsley to
  garnish

Heat the oil in a frying pan, add the veal and fry, turning, until golden brown all over. Add the garlic and onion and cook until they are soft.

Stir in the green pepper, tomatoes, stock and salt and pepper to taste. Transfer to a 1.2 litre (2 pint) casserole dish. Add the bouquet garni. Cover and cook in a preheated moderate oven, 180°C (350°F), Gas Mark 4, for 1 to 1 1/2 hours.

Remove the bouquet garni and skim off any excess fat. Serve hot, garnished with parsley.

Veal Escalopes

2 x 150 g (5 oz)
   veal escalopes
15 g (½ oz) butter
1 teaspoon oil
½ small onion, sliced
50 g (2 oz) button
   mushrooms
2 tablespoons dry
   sherry
4 tablespoons double
   cream
salt and pepper
paprika
TO GARNISH:
2 lemon twists
1 teaspoon chopped
   parsley

Trim the escalopes into neat shapes
and snip the edges to prevent the
meat from curling up.

Heat the butter and oil in a frying
pan, add the onion and fry for 2 to 3
minutes. Add the veal and
mushrooms and cook for 8 to 10
minutes, turning the escalopes once,
until golden brown on both sides.

Stir in the sherry and bring to the
boil. Add the cream and heat
through, stirring. Add salt and
pepper to taste.

Lift the veal escalopes onto a
warmed serving dish and spoon the
sauce over. Sprinkle with paprika to
taste. Garnish each escalope with a
lemon twist and chopped parsley.

37

Piquant Liver

15 g (½ oz) butter
1 small onion,
  chopped
50 g (2 oz) streaky
  bacon, derinded
  and chopped
2 tablespoons plain
  flour
salt and pepper
300 g (10 oz) lambs'
  liver, sliced
50 g (2 oz)
  mushrooms
150 ml (¼ pint)
  stock
1 tablespoon tomato
  purée
¼ teaspoon made
  mustard
2 teaspoons chutney
½ teaspoon sugar
chopped parsley to
  garnish

Melt the butter in a heavy-based pan, add the onion and bacon and fry until soft.

Season the flour with salt and pepper and use to coat the liver. Add to the pan and fry, turning, until evenly browned. Stir in the mushrooms, stock, tomato purée, mustard, chutney and sugar. Add salt and pepper to taste. Bring to the boil, stirring, then cover and simmer for 20 minutes.

Transfer to a warmed serving dish and garnish with parsley. Serve immediately.

Creamed Kidneys with Salami

4-5 lambs' kidneys
15 g (½ oz) butter
1 small onion,
  chopped
25 g (1 oz)
  mushrooms,
  chopped
2 teaspoons plain
  flour
150 ml (¼ pint)
  stock
1-2 tablespoons
  raisins
2 slices salami,
  chopped
salt and pepper
2 tablespoons single
  cream

Remove the skin and core from the kidneys and chop. Melt the butter in a heavy-based pan. Add the onion and fry until soft. Add the kidneys and mushrooms and cook for 2 to 3 minutes. Stir in the flour and cook for 1 minute. Gradually blend in the stock and heat, stirring, until thickened.

Add the raisins, salami and salt and pepper to taste. Cover and simmer for 15 minutes.

Remove from the heat, stir in the cream and serve immediately, with boiled rice.

Celery and Orange Stuffed Hearts

2 lambs' hearts
1 onion, sliced
1 celery stick,
    chopped
15 g (½ oz) butter
150 ml (¼ pint) beef
    stock
STUFFING:
50 g (2 oz) fresh
    white breadcrumbs
½ celery stick, finely
    chopped
grated rind of ½
    orange
½ teaspoon dried
    thyme
salt and pepper
little beaten egg

Remove the fat from the hearts, rinse thoroughly, then drain. Cut out the tubes with scissors.

To make the stuffing: Mix the breadcrumbs, celery, orange rind and thyme with salt and pepper to taste. Bind the mixture with beaten egg.

Fill the hearts with the stuffing, packing it into the cavities firmly. Sew up the openings with string.

Arrange the onion and celery in a 1.2 litre (2 pint) casserole dish. Melt the butter in a frying pan, add the hearts and fry, turning, until evenly browned. Transfer to the casserole. Season the stock to taste and pour over the hearts. Cover and cook in a preheated moderate oven, 180°C (350°F), Gas Mark 4, for 1½ hours or until tender.

Remove the string and serve the hearts, with the sauce, straight from the casserole.

Curried Chicken

15 g (½ oz) butter
1 small onion,
   chopped
½ green pepper,
   cored, seeded and
   chopped
1 tablespoon curry
   powder
2 tablespoons plain
   flour
300 ml (½ pint)
   chicken stock
½ dessert apple,
   cored and chopped
1 tablespoon
   desiccated coconut
1 tablespoon sweet
   chutney
3 tablespoons
   sultanas
salt and pepper
250 g (8 oz) cooked
   chicken, chopped
chopped parsley to
   garnish

Melt the butter in a saucepan, add
the onion and pepper and fry until
soft. Add the curry powder and flour
and continue cooking for 1 minute.
Gradually blend in the stock and
heat, stirring, until thickened.

Stir in the apple, coconut, chutney,
sultanas and salt and pepper to taste.
Cover and simmer for 10 minutes.
Add the chicken and continue
cooking for 20 minutes.

Sprinkle with parsley and serve
hot, with boiled rice.

Peanut and Cumin Chicken

1 tablespoon oil
2 chicken portions
1 small onion, sliced
2 teaspoons plain
  flour
2 teaspoons smooth
  peanut butter
150 ml (¼ pint)
  chicken stock
½ teaspoon cumin
  seeds
salt and pepper
1 tablespoon peanuts,
  chopped, to
  garnish

Heat the oil in a pan, add the chicken and brown on all sides. Drain and transfer to a 1.2 litre (2 pint) casserole dish.

Fry the onion in the oil remaining in the pan until soft. Stir in the flour and peanut butter and cook for 1 minute. Gradually stir in the stock and bring to the boil. Add the cumin and season liberally with salt and pepper.

Pour the sauce over the chicken. Cover and cook in a preheated moderate oven, 180°C (350°F), Gas Mark 4, for 1 to 1¼ hours.

Serve hot, sprinkled with chopped peanuts.

Chicken Maryland

2 tablespoons plain
    flour
salt and pepper
4 chicken drumsticks
1 small egg, beaten
3 tablespoons fresh
    white bread-
    crumbs, toasted
1 tablespoon oil
25 g (1 oz) butter
ACCOMPANIMENTS:
2 rashers streaky
    bacon, derinded
2 bananas
15 g (½ oz) butter
1 x 198 g (7 oz) can
    sweetcorn kernels
TO GARNISH:
watercress sprigs

Season the flour with salt and pepper and use to coat the drumsticks. Dip into the egg, then coat with the breadcrumbs.

Heat the oil and butter in a frying pan, add the chicken and fry, turning, until golden brown all over. Lower the heat, cover and cook gently for 15 to 20 minutes, turning occasionally, until the chicken is tender.

Halve the bacon rashers, roll up and thread onto a skewer. Cook under a preheated hot grill for about 3 minutes.

Cut the bananas in half lengthways. Melt the butter in a pan, add the bananas and fry gently until golden. Heat the sweetcorn in a saucepan, then drain thoroughly.

Drain the chicken and transfer to a warmed serving dish. Arrange the sweetcorn around the chicken and place the bananas and bacon rolls on top.

Garnish with watercress and serve immediately.

Tangy Chicken Salad

3 tablespoons
    sultanas
250 g (8 oz) cooked
    chicken, chopped
1 celery head,
    chopped
½ bunch watercress,
    chopped
juice of ½ orange
150 ml (¼ pint)
    mayonnaise (see
    page 73)
salt and pepper
TO GARNISH:
watercress sprigs
orange segments

Place the sultanas in a bowl and cover with warm water. Leave to soak for 2 hours then drain.

Put the chicken in a bowl with the celery, watercress and sultanas.

Mix the orange juice with the mayonnaise and add salt and pepper to taste. Add to the chicken and mix well.

Pile onto a serving dish and garnish with watercress and orange segments. Serve cold with rice and a green salad.

Chicken and Bacon Pie

15 g (¹/₂ oz) butter
1 small onion,
    chopped
¹/₂ dessert apple,
    peeled, cored and
    chopped
2 tablespoons plain
    flour
150 ml (¹/₄ pint)
    chicken stock
¹/₂ teaspoon dried
    thyme
175 g (6 oz) cooked
    chicken, chopped
50 g (2 oz) cooked
    bacon, chopped
salt and pepper
SHORTCRUST
    PASTRY:
125 g (4 oz) plain
    flour
pinch of salt
25 g (1 oz)
    margarine
25 g (1 oz) lard
1 tablespoon cold
    water
beaten egg to glaze

Melt the butter in a pan, add the onion and apple and fry until soft. Stir in the flour and cook for 1 minute. Gradually blend in the stock and heat, stirring, until thickened. Add the thyme, chicken, bacon and salt and pepper to taste. Transfer to a 600 ml (1 pint) pie dish and place a pie funnel in the centre.

To make the pastry: Sift the flour and salt into a bowl. Rub in the fat until the mixture resembles fine breadcrumbs. Add the water and mix to a firm dough. Knead lightly, then chill for 15 minutes.

Roll out on a floured surface to a circle 3.5 cm (1¹/₂ inches) larger all round than the dish. Cut a 2.5 cm (1 inch) strip from the edge and place on the dampened rim of the dish. Brush with water and put the pastry lid in position, making a hole in the centre for the funnel. Seal, trim and flute the edges. Decorate with pastry leaves made from the trimmings.

Brush with egg and cook in a preheated moderately hot oven, 200°C (400°F), Gas Mark 6, for 20 to 30 minutes. Serve hot.

Apple and Cherry Duckling

15 g (½ oz) butter
2 duckling joints
1 small onion,
chopped
2 teaspoons plain
flour
150 ml (¼ pint)
light stock
2 tablespoons dry
cider (optional)
1 tablespoon
redcurrant jelly
½ teaspoon sugar
salt and pepper
125 g (4 oz) cooking
apples, peeled,
cored and chopped
75 g (3 oz) black
cherries, stoned

Melt the butter in a large saucepan, add the duckling and fry, turning, until evenly browned. Transfer to a 1.75 litre (3 pint) casserole dish, using a slotted spoon.

Fry the onion in the fat remaining in the pan, until soft. Stir in the flour and cook for 1 minute. Gradually blend in the stock and cider, if used. Heat, stirring until thickened. Add the redcurrant jelly and sugar. Season liberally with salt and pepper.

Arrange the apple and cherries on the duckling and pour over the sauce. Cover and cook in a preheated moderate oven, 180°C (350°F), Gas Mark 4, for 1¼ to 1½ hours. Serve hot.

Turkey Fricassée

25 g (1 oz) streaky
  bacon, derinded
  and chopped
1 small onion,
  chopped
1 small carrot, grated
1 celery stick,
  chopped
150 ml (¼ pint)
  light stock
1 bouquet garni
salt and pepper
150 ml (¼ pint)
  milk
  (approximately)
15 g (½ oz) butter
2 tablespoons plain
  flour
grated nutmeg
250 g (8 oz) cooked
  turkey meat,
  chopped
1 tablespoon single
  cream
chopped parsley to
  garnish

Place the bacon, onion, carrot, celery, stock and bouquet garni in a saucepan. Add salt and pepper to taste. Bring to the boil, cover and simmer for 15 minutes.

Strain the stock into a measuring jug and add enough milk to make 300 ml (½ pint) liquor.

Melt the butter in a clean saucepan, stir in the flour and cook for 1 minute. Gradually blend in the liquor and heat, stirring, until thickened. Add nutmeg, salt and pepper to taste.

Stir in the vegetables and turkey meat. Cover and simmer for 15 minutes. Remove from the heat and stir in the cream.

Transfer to a warmed serving dish and sprinkle with parsley. Serve immediately.

Crispy Tuna and Egg

1 x 99 g (3½ oz)
   can tuna, drained
   and flaked
2 tablespoons
   sweetcorn
2 hard-boiled eggs,
   chopped
15 g (½ oz) butter
2 tablespoons plain
   flour
150 ml (¼ pint)
   milk
50 g (2 oz) Cheddar
   cheese, grated
2 teaspoons chopped
   chives
salt and pepper
½ x 25 g (1 oz)
   packet potato
   crisps, crushed
chopped chives to
   garnish

Place the fish in a 600 ml (1 pint) ovenproof dish. Spoon the sweetcorn and egg over the top.

Melt the butter in a saucepan, stir in the flour and cook for 1 minute. Gradually blend in the milk, then heat, stirring, until the sauce thickens. Add the cheese, chives and salt and pepper to taste. Pour over the fish.

Sprinkle the crisps over the top and cook in a preheated moderate oven, 180°C (350°F), Gas Mark 4, for 30 minutes.

Serve hot, garnished with chives.

Farmhouse Omelet

25 g (1 oz) butter
1 onion, diced
1 potato, diced
25 g (1 oz) streaky
   bacon, derinded
   and chopped
25 g (1 oz)
   mushrooms,
   chopped
2 eggs
2 tablespoons milk
1/4 teaspoon dried
   mixed herbs
salt and pepper
50 g (2 oz) Cheddar
   cheese, grated
chopped parsley to
   garnish

Melt the butter in a frying pan, add the onion, potato and bacon and cook gently, turning occasionally, until soft. Add the mushrooms, increase the heat and cook until the vegetables begin to brown.

Beat together the eggs, milk and herbs with salt and pepper to taste. Pour over the vegetables, tilting the pan to spread the mixture evenly. Cook over a moderate heat until the omelet starts to set.

Sprinkle with the cheese and place the frying pan under a preheated hot grill until the cheese is bubbling and golden brown.

Sprinkle with parsley and cut the omelet in half. Lift onto warmed serving plates and serve immediately.

Creamy Onion Quiche

SHORTCRUST
  PASTRY:
75 g (3 oz) plain
  flour
pinch of salt
15 g (½ oz)
  margarine
25 g (1 oz) lard
1 tablespoon cold
  water
FILLING:
15 g (½ oz) butter
175 g (6 oz) onions,
  thinly sliced
2 eggs
114 ml (4 fl oz)
  single cream
salt and pepper
TO GARNISH:
chopped chives

Make and chill the pastry as for
Chicken and Bacon Pie (see page 43).
Roll out and use to line a 15 cm
(6 inch) flan dish.

For the filling: Melt the butter in a
small frying pan, add the onions and
fry until soft. Arrange in the pastry
case. Beat together the eggs and
cream with salt and pepper to taste.
Pour over the onions.

Cook in a preheated moderately
hot oven, 200°C (400°F), Gas Mark
6, for 25 to 35 minutes or until the
filling is set.

Serve hot or cold, garnished with
chives.
2 to 3 servings

Bean and Egg Curry

50 g (2 oz) haricot
  beans
15 g (½ oz) butter
2 rashers streaky
  bacon, derinded
  and chopped
1 onion, chopped
1 celery stick,
  chopped
½-1 teaspoon curry
  powder
¼ teaspoon ground
  ginger
1 tablespoon plain
  flour
150 ml (¼ pint)
  light stock
1 x 227 g (8 oz) can
  tomatoes
salt and pepper
4 hard-boiled eggs
chopped parsley to
  garnish

Place the beans in a bowl, cover with
cold water and leave to soak
overnight.

Drain, rinse and place in a
saucepan. Cover with fresh cold
water, bring to the boil and simmer
for 45 minutes or until tender, then
drain.

Melt the butter in a saucepan, add
the bacon, onion and celery and fry
until soft. Add the curry powder,
ginger and flour and continue to
cook for 1 minute. Gradually blend
in the stock and the tomatoes with
their juice. Heat, stirring until
thickened. Add the beans and salt
and pepper to taste.

Cut the eggs in half lengthways
and add to the curry. Cover and
simmer for about 20 minutes.
Transfer to a warmed serving dish
and garnish with parsley. Serve
immediately.

Savoury Cheese Bake

2 slices bread
15 g (½ oz) butter
2 slices cooked ham,
   chopped
2 tablespoons cooked
   peas
1 egg, beaten
150 ml (¼ pint)
   milk
½ teaspoon made
   mustard
salt and pepper
50 g (2 oz) mature
   Cheddar cheese,
   grated
tomato slices to garnish

Spread the bread with the butter and
cut into triangles. Arrange in the
base of a greased 600 ml (1 pint)
ovenproof dish. Top with the ham
and peas.

Beat together the egg, milk,
mustard and salt and pepper to taste.
Pour into the dish and sprinkle the
cheese on top. Cook in a preheated
moderately hot oven, 190°C (375°F),
Gas Mark 5, for 20 to 25 minutes or
until golden and well risen.

Garnish with tomato slices.
Serve immediately.

Cheese Fondue Anglais

1 small clove garlic, halved
15 g (½ oz) butter
6 tablespoons dry cider
125 g (4 oz) mature Cheddar cheese, grated
125 g (4 oz) Lancashire cheese, crumbled
1 teaspoon cornflour
1 tablespoon brandy
pepper
grated nutmeg
cubes of crusty bread to serve

Rub the inside of a fondue dish, flameproof casserole or saucepan with the cut garlic clove. Add the butter and cider and heat gently. Add the cheeses and cook gently, stirring, until melted.

Blend the cornflour and brandy to a smooth paste. Add pepper and nutmeg to taste and stir into the fondue. Continue to cook for 3 to 4 minutes until smooth and creamy.

To serve: Keep the fondue warm at the table, preferably over a spirit burner. Place the bread on a serving plate. Each person then spears a piece of bread onto a long-handled fondue fork and dips it into the fondue. Serve accompanied by a green salad.

Scone Pizzas

125 g (4 oz) self-raising flour
pinch of dry mustard
salt and pepper
25 g (1 oz) margarine
4 tablespoons milk
TOPPING:
1 x 397 g (14 oz) can tomatoes, drained and chopped
2 teaspoons grated onion
¼ teaspoon dried oregano
¼ teaspoon dried basil
2 slices salami, chopped
125 g (4 oz) Cheddar cheese, grated
6 stuffed olives, sliced

Sift the flour with the mustard, a pinch of salt and pepper to taste into a bowl. Rub in the margarine until the mixture resembles fine bread-crumbs. Stir in the milk and mix to a firm dough. Turn onto a floured surface and knead until smooth.

Divide the dough in half. Roll each piece out to a 15 to 18 cm (6 to 7 inch) circle and place on a large greased baking sheet.

Arrange the tomatoes on top and sprinkle with the onion, herbs and salt and pepper to taste. Sprinkle the salami and cheese over the pizza and top with the olives.

Cook in a preheated moderately hot oven, 200°C (400°F), Gas Mark 6, for 15 to 20 minutes or until the dough is cooked and the cheese is brown and bubbling. Serve warm, with a mixed salad.

Cheese-Topped Savouries

15 g (½ oz) butter
2 rashers streaky
  bacon, derinded
  and chopped
50 g (2 oz)
  mushrooms, sliced
2 tomatoes, skinned
  and chopped
½ teaspoon made
  mustard
salt and pepper
4 slices bread,
  buttered
50 g (2 oz) Cheddar
  cheese, sliced
parsley sprigs to
  garnish

Melt the butter in a pan, add the bacon and fry until soft. Add the mushrooms and tomatoes and cook for 1 minute. Stir in the mustard and salt and pepper to taste.

Divide the mixture between 2 of the bread slices and top with the remaining 2 slices. Toast both sides under a preheated hot grill until golden brown.

Place the cheese on top and return to the grill. Cook until the cheese is golden and bubbling.

Garnish with parsley. Serve immediately.

Vegetable Pasties

Make and chill the pastry as for Chicken and Bacon Pie (see page 43). Divide in half and roll each piece to a 15 cm (6 inch) circle.

Mix together the vegetables, beans, cheese, chutney, most of the egg yolk and salt and pepper to taste. Divide between the pastry circles, leaving a 1 cm (½ inch) border at the edges.

Add a little milk to the remaining egg yolk and use to brush the pastry edges. Fold the pastry in half, enclosing the filling, and press the edges together. Place on a baking sheet.

Make slits in the top and brush the pasties with the remaining egg and milk. Cook in a preheated moderately hot oven, 190°C (375°F), Gas Mark 5, for 20 to 25 minutes.

Serve hot or cold, garnished with parsley.

Cottage Cheese and Spinach Flan

SHORTCRUST
  PASTRY:
75 g (3 oz) plain
  flour
pinch of salt
15 g (½ oz)
  margarine
25 g (1 oz) lard
1 tablespoon cold
  water
FILLING:
125 g (4 oz) frozen
  chopped spinach,
  thawed
salt and pepper
113 g (4 oz) cottage
  cheese, sieved
1 egg, beaten
2 tablespoons fresh
  sour cream
grated nutmeg
25 g (1 oz) Cheddar
  cheese, grated

Make and chill the pastry as for
Chicken and Bacon Pie (see page 43).
Roll out and use to line a 15 cm
(6 inch) flan dish or tin, standing on
a baking sheet.

Drain the spinach thoroughly and
place in the pastry case. Sprinkle
with salt and pepper.

Mix together the cottage cheese,
egg, sour cream and salt, pepper and
nutmeg to taste. Pour over the
spinach and sprinkle with the grated
cheese.

Cook in a preheated moderately
hot oven, 200°C (400°F), Gas Mark
6, for 25 to 35 minutes or until the
filling is set. Serve hot or cold.
2 to 3 servings

53

Cheese Pots

40 g (1½ oz) blue
Stilton cheese
25 g (1 oz) butter,
softened
50 g (2 oz) Cheddar
cheese, finely
grated
2 tablespoons milk
1 small clove garlic,
crushed
1 teaspoon chopped
chives
salt and pepper
parsley sprigs to
garnish

Place the Stilton and butter in a bowl
and beat until thoroughly blended.
Beat in the Cheddar cheese and milk.
Add the garlic, chives and salt and
pepper to taste.

Divide the mixture between 2 small
serving pots or dishes and chill
before serving. Garnish with parsley
and serve with hot toast.

Cheese Medley Coleslaw

125 g (4 oz) white
    cabbage, finely
    shredded
1 carrot, grated
1 celery stick,
    chopped
25 g (1 oz) Edam
    cheese, diced
25 g (1 oz) Double
    Gloucester cheese,
    diced
25 g (1 oz) blue
    Stilton cheese,
    diced
2 tablespoons natural
    low-fat yogurt
2 tablespoons
    mayonnaise (see
    page 73)
salt and pepper
chopped parsley to
    garnish

Place the vegetables and cheeses in a serving bowl and mix together.

Combine the yogurt and mayonnaise with salt and pepper to taste. Pour over the salad and toss well.

Sprinkle with parsley. Serve with crusty rolls and butter.

Stilton Cauliflower

1 small cauliflower,
    divided into florets
salt and pepper
15 g (½ oz) butter
2 tablespoons plain
    flour
150 ml (¼ pint)
    milk
40 g (1½ oz) blue
    Stilton cheese,
    crumbled
1 tablespoon dry
    breadcrumbs

Cook the cauliflower in boiling salted water for about 12 minutes until tender. Drain and transfer to a warmed ovenproof serving dish.

Melt the butter in a saucepan, stir in the flour and continue cooking for 1 minute. Gradually blend in the milk and heat, stirring, until thickened.

Stir in the cheese and heat gently, stirring, until melted. Add salt and pepper to taste.

Pour the sauce over the cauliflower and top with the bread-crumbs. Place under a preheated medium grill until the topping is golden brown. Serve hot.

Caraway Cabbage

350 g (12 oz) red or
    white cabbage,
    shredded
1 small onion,
    chopped
1/2 teaspoon caraway
    seeds
salt and pepper
15 g (1/2 oz) butter
1/2 red pepper, cored,
    seeded and sliced

Place the cabbage, onion and
caraway seeds in a pan of boiling
salted water. Cook for 5 to 10
minutes, drain and return to the pan.

Add the butter and red pepper and
toss the ingredients over a low heat
for 1 minute. Add salt and pepper to
taste and transfer to a warmed
serving dish. Serve immediately.

Vegetarian Hotpot

25 g (1 oz) dried
   chick peas
25 g (1 oz) dried
   haricot beans
25 g (1 oz) dried
   black-eyed beans
25 g (1 oz) dried red
   kidney beans
15 g (½ oz) butter
1 small onion,
   chopped
1 carrot, sliced
1 celery stick,
   chopped
1 clove garlic,
   crushed
1 x 227 g (8 oz) can
   tomatoes
½ teaspoon dried
   mixed herbs
salt and pepper
75 g (3 oz) Cheddar
   cheese, grated

Place the chick peas, haricot beans and black-eyed beans in a bowl and cover with cold water. Place the kidney beans in a separate bowl and cover with water. Leave to soak overnight.

Drain and place the chick peas, haricot beans and black-eyed beans in a saucepan; put the kidney beans in a separate pan (to avoid tinting the others pink). Cover the pulses with fresh cold water. Bring to the boil and boil steadily for 10 minutes. Lower the heat, cover and simmer for 40 minutes or until tender. Drain, rinse under cold water, then drain.

Melt the butter in a saucepan, add the onion, carrot and celery and fry until soft. Stir in the garlic, pulses, tomatoes with their juice, herbs and salt and pepper to taste.

Bring to the boil, cover and simmer for 1 to 1¼ hours, adding a little water if the mixture becomes dry. Check the seasoning. Transfer to a warmed serving dish. Sprinkle with the cheese. Serve immediately.

Spiced Vegetables and Rice

1 tablespoon oil
2 leeks, sliced
1 carrot, thinly sliced
1 onion, sliced
½ dessert apple,
  cored and chopped
½ teaspoon cumin
  seeds
½ teaspoon ground
  coriander
pinch of cayenne
  pepper
salt and pepper
4-5 tablespoons stock
75 g (3 oz) brown
  rice
chopped parsley to
  garnish

Heat the oil in a saucepan, add the leeks, carrot, onion and apple and cook gently, stirring, for 3 minutes. Add the cumin, coriander, cayenne and salt and pepper to taste. Continue to cook for 3 minutes, then stir in the stock. Cover and simmer for 10 to 15 minutes until the vegetables are tender but not soft.

Cook the rice in plenty of boiling salted water for 45 to 50 minutes or until tender. Drain and rinse with boiling water.

Stir the rice into the vegetables and heat gently for 5 minutes. Transfer to a warmed serving dish and garnish with parsley. Serve hot.

Mediterranean Vegetables

1 small aubergine
salt and pepper
1 ½ tablespoons oil
1 small onion, sliced
1 small clove garlic,
  crushed
1 celery stick,
  chopped
½ green pepper,
  cored, seeded and
  chopped
2 tomatoes, skinned
  and chopped
2 tablespoons water
½ teaspoon dried
  oregano
½ teaspoon dried
  basil
chopped parsley to
  garnish

Cut the aubergine into thin slices and sprinkle with salt. Place in a colander and leave for 30 minutes. Rinse and pat dry with kitchen paper.

Heat the oil in a saucepan and add the aubergine, onion, garlic, celery and green pepper. Cook, stirring, until all the vegetables are coated with oil. Cover and cook for 10 minutes.

Add the tomatoes, water, oregano, basil and salt and pepper to taste. Bring to the boil, cover and simmer for 30 minutes.

Serve hot or cold, sprinkled with parsley.

Minted Courgettes with Peas and Corn

175 g (6 oz)
    courgettes, thinly
    sliced
salt
50 g (2 oz) frozen
    peas
50 g (2 oz) frozen
    sweetcorn
2 mint sprigs
15 g (½ oz) butter
2 teaspoons chopped
    chives

Place the courgettes in a pan of boiling salted water. Add the peas, sweetcorn and mint. Cover and simmer for 5 to 6 minutes until the vegetables are just tender. Drain, remove the mint and return the vegetables to the pan.

Add the butter and chives and toss over a low heat for 1 minute. Transfer to a warmed serving dish. Serve hot.

Peas French-Style

1 x 227 g (8 oz)
   packet frozen peas
3 lettuce leaves,
   shredded
25 g (1 oz) butter
3 spring onions,
   finely chopped
½ teaspoon sugar
4 tablespoons light
   stock
1 sprig each parsley
   and mint, tied
   together
salt and pepper

Place all the ingredients in a saucepan, adding salt and pepper to taste. Bring slowly to the boil, cover and simmer for 15 to 20 minutes or until the peas are tender, adding more stock or water if necessary.

Discard the parsley and mint. Transfer to a serving dish. Serve immediately.

Layered Potatoes with Sour Cream

350 g (12 oz)
    potatoes, thinly
    sliced
1 small onion, finely
    chopped
4 tablespoons fresh
    sour cream
salt and pepper
40 g (1½ oz) butter
4 tablespoons milk
chopped chives to
    garnish

Line the base of a greased 600 ml
(1 pint) ovenproof dish with potato
slices. Add a little of the onion and
sour cream. Sprinkle liberally with
salt and pepper. Repeat the layers
until all these ingredients are used,
finishing with a layer of potato.

Melt 25 g (1 oz) of the butter in a
saucepan, stir in the milk and pour
over the potatoes. Dot the remaining
butter on top.

Cover and cook in a preheated
moderately hot oven, 190°C (375°F),
Gas Mark 5, for 45 minutes.
Uncover and cook for a further
20 minutes or until the potatoes are
golden brown.

Garnish with chives. Serve hot
with lamb chops or sausages and
bacon.

Baked Courgettes

15 g (½ oz) butter
1 small onion,
    chopped
250 g (8 oz)
    courgettes, sliced
1 large tomato,
    skinned and sliced
½ teaspoon dried
    oregano
salt and pepper
1 egg, beaten
50 g (2 oz) Gruyère
    cheese, grated
parsley sprigs to
    garnish

Melt the butter in a saucepan, add
the onion and courgettes and fry for
2 minutes. Transfer to a shallow
ovenproof dish and place the tomato
slices on top. Sprinkle with the
oregano and salt and pepper to taste.

Mix together the egg, cheese and
salt and pepper to taste. Spoon over
the tomato. Cook in a preheated
moderate oven, 180°C (350°F), Gas
Mark 4, for 15 to 20 minutes until
the topping is golden.

Garnish with parsley. Serve hot.

Savoury Stuffed Peppers

2 medium green
   peppers
salt and pepper
15 g (½ oz) butter
½ small onion,
   finely chopped
2 rashers streaky
   bacon, derinded
   and chopped
50 g (2 oz)
   long-grain rice,
   cooked
50 g (2 oz) Cheddar
   cheese, grated
4 tablespoons single
   cream
¼ teaspoon made
   mustard
1 teaspoon chopped
   parsley

Cut the tops from the peppers and reserve; discard the seeds and cores. Blanch in boiling salted water for 2 minutes, remove and drain.

Melt the butter in a saucepan, add the onion and bacon and fry until soft. Remove from the heat and stir in the rice and cheese.

Beat the cream with the mustard, parsley and salt and pepper to taste, then stir into the rice mixture. Pile this mixture into the pepper shells. Replace the tops.

Place in a shallow ovenproof dish, cover with foil and cook in a preheated moderate oven, 180°C (350°F), Gas Mark 4, for 15 to 20 minutes. Serve hot.

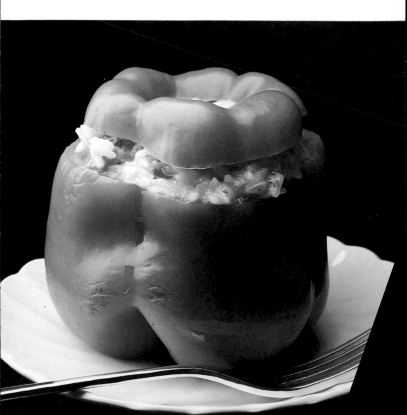

Bean Sprout Salad

125 g (4 oz) fresh
bean sprouts
1 celery stick,
chopped
1 carrot, grated
2.5 cm (1 inch) piece
of cucumber, cut in
strips
3 tablespoons raisins
1 tablespoon French
dressing (see page
73)
1 tablespoon natural
low-fat yogurt
salt and pepper

Place the bean sprouts, celery, carrot,
cucumber and raisins in a bowl.

Combine the French dressing with
the yogurt. Season with salt and
pepper to taste. Pour over the salad
and toss well. Serve with meat or
fish.

Onion and Avocado Salad

50 g (2 oz) streaky
  bacon, derinded
½ avocado pear,
  stoned
2 teaspoons lemon
  juice
3 crisp lettuce leaves,
  shredded
2 spring onions,
  chopped
25 g (1 oz) salted
  peanuts
2 tablespoons French
  dressing (see page
  73)
salt and pepper

Cook the bacon under a preheated medium grill until crisp. Chop into small pieces and leave to cool.

Peel and slice the avocado. Place in a serving bowl and sprinkle with the lemon juice. Add the lettuce, spring onions, bacon, peanuts and French dressing. Toss well and season with salt and pepper to taste. Chill before serving.

Fruit Coleslaw

1 red-skinned dessert
   apple, cored and
   chopped
2 teaspoons lemon
   juice
125 g (4 oz) white
   cabbage, finely
   shredded
1 small carrot, grated
50 g (2 oz) dates,
   stoned and
   chopped
1 tablespoon sultanas
50 g (2 oz) green
   grapes, halved and
   seeded
2 tablespoons natural
   low-fat yogurt
2 tablespoons
   mayonnaise (see
   page 73)
salt and pepper

Place the apple in a bowl, sprinkle
with the lemon juice and toss well.
Add the cabbage, carrot, dates,
sultanas and grapes.

Mix together the yogurt,
mayonnaise and salt and pepper to
taste. Pour over the salad and toss
well. Pile into a serving dish.

Cheese-Filled Avocado

1 avocado pear
1 teaspoon lemon
    juice
50 g (2 oz) Danish
    blue cheese
2 tablespoons curd
    cheese
salt and pepper
parsley sprigs to
    garnish

Halve the avocado, remove the stone and scoop out some of the flesh, leaving 1 cm (½ inch) thick shells. Reserve the shells.

Place the avocado flesh and lemon juice in a bowl and mash, using a fork. Blend in the cheeses and salt and pepper to taste.

Pile the mixture into the avocado shells. Serve chilled, garnished with parsley.

Orange Pasta Salad

125 g (4 oz) pasta
    shells
salt and pepper
50 g (2 oz) canned
    red kidney beans,
    drained
½ green pepper,
    cored, seeded and
    chopped
2 teaspoons chopped
    parsley
grated rind and juice
    of ½ orange
1 tablespoon French
    dressing (see page
    73)

Cook the pasta in plenty of boiling
salted water until just tender. Drain
and rinse under cold running water.

Place the pasta in a serving bowl.
Add the kidney beans, pepper,
parsley and orange rind. Mix the
orange juice with the French dressing
and add salt and pepper to taste.
Pour over the salad and toss well.
Chill before serving.

Creamy Potato Salad

250 g (8 oz) boiled
  potatoes, diced
few watercress sprigs,
  chopped
25 g (1 oz) cooked
  ham, chopped
4 tablespoons double
  cream
1 teaspoon made
  mustard
pinch of sugar
salt and pepper
watercress sprigs to
  garnish

Place the potatoes (preferably while still warm) in a bowl and add the chopped watercress and ham.

Lightly whip the cream with the mustard, sugar and salt and pepper to taste. Add to the potatoes and mix well.

Pile into a serving dish. Leave in a cool place for at least 30 minutes before serving to allow the potatoes to absorb the dressing.

Garnish with watercress and serve with cold meats.

Apple and Nut Salad

2 dessert apples,
cored and chopped
2 teaspoons lemon
juice
2 celery sticks,
chopped
25 g (1 oz) salted
peanuts
25 g (1 oz) walnuts,
chopped
3 tablespoons
mayonnaise (see
page 73)
few lettuce leaves
paprika to garnish

Place the apples in a bowl, sprinkle with lemon juice and toss well. Add the remaining ingredients, except the lettuce; mix well.

Line a serving dish with lettuce leaves, pile the salad on top and sprinkle with paprika to garnish.

French Dressing

3 teaspoons French
mustard
1/2 teaspoon sugar
1 teaspoon each
finely chopped
chives and parsley
5 tablespoons vinegar
10 tablespoons salad
or olive oil
salt and pepper

Mix together the mustard, sugar and herbs. Stir in the vinegar. Transfer to a screw-top jar and add the oil and salt and pepper to taste. Shake vigourously to blend before serving.
Makes about 300 ml (1/2 pint)

Mayonnaise

2 egg yolks
1/2 teaspoon salt
1/2 teaspoon pepper
1/2 teaspoon dry
mustard
1 teaspoon caster
sugar
1/2 pint salad or olive
oil
1 1/2 tablespoons
white vinegar or
lemon juice

Make sure that all the ingredients are at room temperature.

Beat the egg yolks in a bowl with the salt, pepper, mustard and sugar. Add the oil, drop by drop, beating constantly. As the mayonnaise thickens the oil may be added in a thin stream.

When all of the oil has been added, gradually add the vinegar and mix thoroughly.
Makes about 300 ml (1/2 pint)

DESSERTS

Raspberry Soufflé Omelet

4 tablespoons stewed
    raspberries
4 eggs, separated
2 tablespoons caster
    sugar
2 tablespoons water
pinch of salt
TO FINISH:
few fresh raspberries
sifted icing sugar

Place the raspberries in a greased shallow ovenproof dish.

Whisk the egg yolks and sugar together until pale. Stir in the water.

Whisk the egg whites with the salt until stiff, then fold into the egg yolks. Pour over the raspberries and cook in a preheated moderate oven, 180°C (350°F), Gas Mark 4, for 15 to 20 minutes.

Top with the raspberries and sprinkle with icing sugar. Serve immediately, with cream.

Gooseberry and Hazelnut Brulée

250 g (8 oz)
  gooseberries
25-50 g (1-2 oz)
  sugar
150 g (5 oz)
  hazelnut yogurt
1 tablespoon soft
  dark brown sugar

Place the gooseberries in a saucepan with sugar to taste. Cook gently, stirring, until the juices run, then cover and simmer until tender.

Spoon into individual heatproof dishes and leave to cool. Top with the yogurt and chill well.

Just before serving, sprinkle with brown sugar and place under a preheated hot grill for 1 to 2 minutes. Serve immediately.

Baked Bananas

2 bananas, thickly
  sliced
2 teaspoons lemon
  juice
25 g (1 oz) dates,
  chopped
2 teaspoons honey
1 tablespoon water
1-2 tablespoons
  chopped walnuts

Place the bananas in a 450 ml
(³/4 pint) ovenproof dish, add the
lemon juice and toss well. Sprinkle
the dates over the top.

Blend together the honey and
water and spoon over the bananas.
Top with the walnuts. Cover with
foil and cook in a preheated
moderate oven, 180°C (350°F), Gas
Mark 4, for 20 minutes. Serve hot,
with cream.

Date and Lemon Pudding

3 slices buttered
  wholemeal bread,
  crusts removed and
  quartered
40 g (1½ oz) dates,
  stoned and
  chopped
1 egg
2 tablespoons soft
  brown sugar
1 teaspoon finely
  grated lemon rind
¼ teaspoon ground
  mixed spice
300 ml (½ pint)
  milk

Arrange the bread in a greased
600 ml (1 pint) ovenproof dish.
Sprinkle the dates over the top.

Beat together the egg, 1 tablespoon
of the sugar, the lemon rind and
spice. Heat the milk, but do not boil;
stir into the egg mixture.

Strain the custard over the bread
and leave for 10 to 15 minutes. Stand
the dish in a roasting pan, containing
enough water to come halfway up
the dish. Cook in a preheated
moderate oven, 180°C (350°F), Gas
Mark 4, for 25 to 30 minutes or until
the custard is just set.

Sprinkle with the remaining sugar
and serve immediately.

Spiced Apple Amber

250 g (8 oz) cooking
  apples, peeled,
  cored and sliced
2 teaspoons honey
¼ teaspoon ground
  cinnamon
¼ teaspoon grated
  nutmeg
1 tablespoon water
1 egg, separated
25 g (1 oz) caster
  sugar

Place the apples, honey, cinnamon,
nutmeg and water in a saucepan.
Heat gently until the apples are tender.
Cool slightly, then sieve or purée in
an electric blender. Beat in the egg
yolk, then spoon into a buttered
600 ml (1 pint) ovenproof dish.

Whisk the egg white until stiff, then
whisk in half the sugar. Fold in the
remainder and spoon over the apples.

Cook in a preheated moderate oven,
180°C (350°F), Gas Mark 4, for 10 to
15 minutes. Serve hot, with cream.

Banana Splits with Fudge Sauce

2 bananas
4 tablespoons vanilla
   ice cream
4 tablespoons double
   cream, whipped
2 teaspoons chopped
   nuts
1 glacé cherry,
   halved
SAUCE:
15 g (½ oz) plain
   chocolate
1 tablespoon warm
   water
50 g (2 oz) soft
   brown sugar
1 teaspoon golden
   syrup
2-3 drops vanilla
   essence

Cut the bananas in half lengthways and sandwich the halves together with the ice cream. Place on individual serving plates. Spoon or pipe the cream on top and decorate with the nuts and cherry pieces.

To make the sauce: Melt the chocolate with the water in a basin standing over a pan of hot water.

Transfer to a saucepan and add the sugar and syrup. Heat gently, stirring, until the sugar has dissolved. Bring to the boil and boil steadily, without stirring, for 3 to 4 minutes. Remove from the heat and stir in the vanilla.

Pour the sauce over the banana splits or hand separately.

Spicy Orange Creamed Rice

25 g (1 oz) pudding
   rice
150 ml (¼ pint)
   water
300 ml (½ pint)
   milk
25 g (1 oz) soft
   brown sugar
1 teaspoon finely
   grated orange rind
¼ teaspoon grated
   nutmeg
1-2 tablespoons
   sultanas
1 bay leaf
15 g (½ oz) butter

Place the rice in a saucepan with the water. Bring to the boil, cover and simmer for 10 minutes. Drain and place the rice in a 600 ml (1 pint) ovenproof dish. Add the remaining ingredients.

Cook in a preheated moderate oven, 160°C (325°F), Gas Mark 3, for 1½ to 2 hours, stirring twice during the first hour to incorporate the skin and increase the creaminess. Serve hot or cold.

Plum Tart

125 g (4 oz) plain
  flour
pinch of salt
1 teaspoon caster
  sugar
75 g (3 oz) butter
1 egg, beaten
FILLING:
250 g (8 oz) red
  plums, halved and
  stoned
150 ml (¼ pint)
  water
50 g (2 oz) sugar
2 teaspoons cornflour
TO FINISH:
sifted icing sugar

Sift the flour and salt into a bowl and add the sugar. Rub in the butter until the mixture resembles breadcrumbs. Add the egg and mix to a smooth dough. Knead lightly, cover and chill for 30 minutes.

Roll out the dough on a floured surface and use to line a 15 cm (6 inch) flan ring placed on a baking sheet. Reserve the trimmings.

Put the plums, water and sugar in a saucepan. Cook gently until tender. Drain, reserving the juice.

Blend the cornflour with a little cooled juice, then add the remainder. Bring to the boil, stirring. Add the plums and spoon into the pastry case. Cut strips from the pastry trimmings and make a lattice pattern over the filling.

Cook in a preheated moderately hot oven, 200°C (400°F), Gas Mark 6, for 25 minutes. Cool in the tin.

When cold, transfer to a serving plate and sprinkle with icing sugar.
2 to 3 servings

Banana Orange Caramel

1 banana, sliced
1 pear, peeled, cored
   and sliced
pinch of ground
   cinnamon
grated rind and juice
   of ½ orange
1 tablespoon water
25 g (1 oz) sugar
2 eggs, beaten
toasted almonds to
   decorate

Place the banana, pear, cinnamon, orange rind and juice in a saucepan and simmer for 5 minutes. Remove from the heat and leave to cool.

Place the water and sugar in a saucepan and heat gently until dissolved. Bring to the boil and boil steadily until a rich golden brown caramel is formed. Pour into buttered dariole moulds or individual dishes.

Strain the eggs over the fruit and stir well. Pour into the moulds.

Place in a roasting pan containing enough water to come halfway up the dishes. Cook in a preheated cool oven, 150°C (300°F), Gas Mark 2, for 25 to 30 minutes or until just firm.

Leave in the refrigerator overnight. Just before serving, turn out and sprinkle with almonds. Serve with cream.

Chocolate and Orange Mousse

50 g (2 oz) plain
   chocolate
knob of butter
grated rind and juice
   of ½ orange
1 egg, separated
4 tablespoons double
   cream, whipped
chocolate curls to
   decorate (see note)

Melt the chocolate in a basin over a pan of hot water. Remove from the heat and add the butter, orange rind and juice, and the egg yolk. Beat until smooth. Leave to cool.

Fold in the whipped cream. Whisk the egg white until just firm and fold into the chocolate mixture. Pour into individual serving dishes. Chill in the refrigerator until set.

Decorate with the chocolate curls before serving.

NOTE: To make chocolate curls, shave slivers from a chocolate block, using a potato peeler.

Ginger and Nut Ice Cream

150 ml (¼ pint)
  double cream
1 tablespoon milk
2 tablespoons icing
  sugar, sifted
25 g (1 oz)
  preserved ginger,
  finely chopped
2 teaspoons ginger
  syrup
1-2 tablespoons
  finely chopped
  hazelnuts

Place the cream and milk in a bowl
and whip lightly. Fold in the icing
sugar. Pour into a shallow freezer
tray, cover and freeze for about
45 minutes, until the ice cream has
frozen around the sides of the tray.

Turn into a chilled bowl and
whisk until smooth. Stir in the
ginger, syrup and hazelnuts.

Return the ice cream to the tray,
cover and freeze until firm.

Transfer to the refrigerator about
20 minutes before serving to soften.
Scoop into individual dishes. Serve
with crisp biscuits if liked.

Melon and Orange with Mint

½ small honeydew
  melon
1 orange
few mint leaves,
  crushed
mint sprigs to
  decorate

Remove the pips from the melon,
cut the flesh from the skin and chop
into pieces. Place in a bowl.

Grate the rind from the orange and
add to the melon. Peel and segment
the orange, discarding all the pith.
Add to the melon with the crushed
mint. Mix well and pile into
individual serving dishes. Chill
before serving.

Decorate with mint sprigs and
serve with cream or ice cream.

Crunchy Apples

250 g (8 oz) cooking
   apples, peeled,
   cored and sliced
25 g (1 oz)
   granulated sugar
1 teaspoon lemon
   juice
1 tablespoon water
1/4 teaspoon ground
   cinnamon
20 g (3/4 oz) butter
40 g (1 1/2 oz)
   porridge oats
1 tablespoon brown
   sugar
4 tablespoons double
   cream
2 teaspoons milk
grated chocolate to
   decorate

Place the apples in a saucepan with
the granulated sugar, lemon juice,
water and cinnamon. Cook gently
until the fruit is soft. Beat to a pulp
with a wooden spoon, then transfer
to individual glass serving dishes.

Melt the butter in a saucepan and
add the porridge oats and brown
sugar. Heat gently, stirring, until the
oats are browned; leave to cool.
Spoon over the apples.

Whip the cream and milk together
lightly and spoon over the topping.
Decorate with chocolate.

Apricot and Chocolate Dessert

2 thick slices choco-
    late Swiss roll
4 canned apricot
    halves
4 tablespoons apricot
    yogurt
4 tablespoons double
    cream, whipped
grated chocolate to
    decorate

Place the Swiss roll in individual
serving dishes. Drain the apricots
and use a little of the juice to moisten
the Swiss roll. Chop the apricots and
spoon over the Swiss roll.

Fold the yogurt into the cream,
spoon over the apricots and decorate
with grated chocolate. Serve chilled.

Blackcurrant Syllabub

125 g (4 oz)
  blackcurrants
25 g (1 oz)
  granulated sugar
grated rind and juice
  of ½ lemon
1 tablespoon sherry
114 ml (4 fl oz)
  double cream
1 tablespoon caster
  sugar

Place the blackcurrants, granulated sugar, lemon rind and juice in a saucepan and cook gently for 5 minutes. Cool slightly, then purée in an electric blender or rub through a sieve. Stir in the sherry.

Place the cream, caster sugar and half the blackcurrant purée in a bowl and whisk until the mixture forms soft peaks.

Spoon the remaining purée into the base of 2 glasses and top with the cream mixture. Chill before serving, with sponge fingers if liked.

NOTE: Any soft fruit can be used instead of blackcurrants.

Pineapple Freeze

½ *fresh pineapple*
1-2 tablespoons
  water
50 g (2 oz) icing
  sugar, sifted
mint sprigs to
  decorate

Cut the flesh from the pineapple,
discarding the central core; reserve
the shell. Chop and place in an
electric blender. Add a little water
and work to a purée. Stir in the icing
sugar.

 Pile the mixture into the reserved
shell, cover and freeze until firm.

 Transfer to the refrigerator
20 minutes before serving to soften
slightly. Decorate with mint sprigs.

Apricot and Banana Cream

50 g (2 oz) dried
   apricots
2 ripe bananas
1 teaspoon lemon
   juice
4 tablespoons double
   cream
2 tablespoons natural
   low-fat yogurt
2 teaspoons honey
2 walnut halves to
   decorate

Place the apricots in a bowl and pour over cold water to cover. Leave to soak for a few hours; drain.

Place the bananas in an electric blender with the apricots, lemon juice, cream, yogurt and honey. Blend to a smooth cream.

Spoon into individual glass serving dishes and chill before serving. Decorate with walnut halves.

Coffee Junket

300 ml (½ pint)
  milk
1 teaspoon caster
  sugar
1 teaspoon instant
  coffee powder
½ teaspoon rennet
  essence
2 walnut pieces to
  decorate

Place the milk, sugar and coffee in a saucepan. Heat gently, stirring to dissolve the coffee and sugar, until the mixture reaches 36°C (97°F) or 'blood heat'.

Stir in the rennet and pour into individual serving bowls. Leave at room temperature for 1½ hours or until set.

Chill before serving. Decorate with walnut pieces.

Quick Rhubarb Fool

250 g (8 oz)
  rhubarb, chopped
1 tablespoon water
grated rind of
  ½ orange
40 g (1½ oz) sugar
114 ml (4 fl oz)
  double cream,
  whipped
4 tablespoons
  raspberry yogurt

Place the rhubarb in a saucepan with the water, orange rind and sugar. Cook gently until soft. Leave to cool, then purée in an electric blender or rub through a sieve.

Fold two-thirds of the cream into the rhubarb with the yogurt. Spoon into individual glass dishes and pipe whirls of cream on top. Chill before serving.

Orange Cheesecake

25 g (1 oz) butter
50 g (2 oz) digestive
  biscuits, crushed
FILLING:
113 g (4 oz) curd
  cheese
25 g (1 oz) caster
  sugar
grated rind and juice
  of ½ orange
114 ml (4 fl oz)
  double cream,
  whipped
mandarin oranges to
  decorate

Melt the butter and stir in the crushed biscuits. Press the mixture onto the base and sides of a 15 cm (6 inch) flan dish. Leave in the refrigerator until firm.

Mix the curd cheese with the sugar, orange rind and juice. Fold in two-thirds of the cream. Spoon the mixture into the biscuit flan case.

Decorate with the remaining cream and mandarin oranges. Chill before serving.
2 to 3 servings

Summer Fruits and Sour Cream Dessert

25 g (1 oz) sugar
4 tablespoons water
175 g (6 oz) red
   plums, stoned
125 g (4 oz)
   raspberries
4 tablespoons fresh
   sour cream
2 teaspoons brown
   sugar

Place the sugar and water in a saucepan and heat gently until dissolved. Increase the heat and boil steadily for 2 minutes. Allow to cool, then chill.

Cut the plums into slices. Divide the plums and raspberries between individual serving dishes and pour over the syrup.

Spoon the sour cream over the fruit and sprinkle with brown sugar. Serve chilled.

Apple and Pear Ginger Trifle

1 medium cooking
    apple, peeled,
    cored and sliced
1 medium pear,
    peeled, cored and
    sliced
4 tablespoons cider
25 g (1 oz) soft
    brown sugar
¼ teaspoon ground
    ginger
3 slices ginger cake,
    cut in half
6 tablespoons
    whipping cream
2 teaspoons icing
    sugar, sifted
1 tablespoon chopped
    nuts, toasted

Place the apple and pear in a
saucepan with the cider, brown sugar
and ginger. Cook gently until the
fruit is just tender. Leave to cool.

Arrange the cake in individual
glass serving dishes and spoon the
fruit and cooking liquid over the top.

Lightly whip the cream and fold in
the icing sugar. Spoon over the fruit
and sprinkle with the nuts. Serve
chilled.

INDEX